D1257226

Presented to:

_____

From:

_____

Date:

_____

Jesus Calling®

50 Devotions for Comfort

Sarah Young

THOMAS NELSON
Since 1798

Published in Nashville, Tennessee, by Thomas Nelson. Thomas Nelson is a registered trademark of HarperCollins Christian Publishing, Inc.

Unless otherwise noted, Scripture quotations are taken from the Holy Bible, New International Version®, NIV®. Copyright © 1973, 1978, 1984 by Biblica, Inc.® Used by permission of Zondervan. All rights reserved worldwide. www.zondervan.com. The "NIV" and "New International Version" are trademarks registered in the United States Patent and Trademark Office by Biblica, Inc.®

Scripture quotations marked AMP are from the Amplified® Bible. Copyright © 1954, 1958, 1962, 1964, 1965, 1987 by The Lockman Foundation. Used by permission. (www.Lockman.org)

Scripture quotations marked ESV are from the ESV® Bible (The Holy Bible, English Standard Version®). Copyright © 2001 by Crossway, a publishing ministry of Good News Publishers. Used by permission. All rights reserved.

Scripture quotations marked KJV are from the King James Version. Public domain.

Scripture quotations marked NASB are from New American Standard Bible®. Copyright © 1960, 1962, 1963, 1968, 1971, 1972, 1973, 1975, 1977, 1995 by The Lockman Foundation. Used by permission. (www.Lockman.org)

Scripture quotations marked NKJV are from the New King James Version®. © 1982 by Thomas Nelson. Used by permission. All rights reserved.

Any Internet addresses, phone numbers, or company or product information printed in this book are offered as a resource and are not intended in any way to be or to imply an endorsement by Thomas Nelson, nor does Thomas Nelson vouch for the existence, content, or services of these sites, phone numbers, companies, or products beyond the life of this book.

ISBN 978-1-4003-1090-6

The Library of Congress has cataloged the earlier edition as follows:

Young, Sarah, 1946–
Jesus Calling / by Sarah Young.
p. cm.
ISBN 978-1-59145-188-4 (hardcover)
1. Devotional calendars. 2. Devotional literature, English. I. Title.
BV4811.Y675 2004
242'.2—dc22   2044005474

Printed in China

18 19 20 21 22 TIMS 5 4 3 2

INTRODUCTION

To someone on the verge of losing hope, I stress the importance of trusting God in the dark—when you're deeply disappointed and cannot understand His ways. I encourage you to grasp on to Jesus and to His Word, memorizing portions of Scripture that are especially meaningful to you.

The devotions in this book are meant to be read slowly, preferably in a quiet place—with your Bible open. The Bible is the only infallible, inerrant Word of God, and I endeavor to keep my writings consistent with that unchanging standard. I have written from the perspective of Jesus speaking, to help readers feel more personally connected with Him. So the first person singular ("I," "Me," "My," "Mine") always refers to Christ; "you" refers to you, the reader. Scripture references are included after each daily reading. Words from the Scriptures (some paraphrased, some quoted) are indicated in italics and are interwoven into each entry.

Remember that Jesus is Immanuel, *God with us*. May you enjoy His Presence in ever-increasing measure.

Sarah Young

COME TO ME with all your weaknesses: physical, emotional, and spiritual. Rest in the comfort of My Presence, remembering that *nothing is impossible with Me*.

Pry your mind away from your problems so you can focus your attention on Me. Recall that I am *able to do immeasurably more than all you ask or imagine*. Instead of trying to direct Me to do this and that, seek to attune yourself to what I am *already* doing.

When anxiety attempts to wedge its way into your thoughts, remind yourself that *I am your Shepherd*. The bottom line is that I am taking care of you; therefore, you needn't be afraid of anything. Rather than trying to maintain control over your life, abandon yourself to My will. Though this may feel frightening—even dangerous—the safest place to be is in My will.

LUKE 1:37; EPHESIANS 3:20–21; PSALM 23:1–4

The LORD is my *shepherd*,

I shall not be in want. He makes me

lie down in green pastures, he leads

me beside quiet waters, he restores

my soul. He guides me in paths

of *righteousness*

for his name's sake. Even though

I walk through the valley of the

shadow of death, I will fear no evil,

for you are with me; your rod and

your staff, they comfort me.

—PSALM 23:1-4

DON'T BE SO HARD ON YOURSELF. I can bring good even out of your mistakes. Your finite mind tends to look backward, longing to undo decisions you have come to regret. This is a waste of time and energy, leading only to frustration. Instead of floundering in the past, release your mistakes to Me. Look to Me in trust, anticipating that My infinite creativity can weave both good choices and bad into a lovely design.

Because you are human, you will continue to make mistakes. Thinking that you should live an error-free life is symptomatic of pride. Your failures can be a source of blessing, humbling you and giving you empathy for other people in their weaknesses. Best of all, failure highlights your dependence on Me. I am able to bring beauty out of the morass of your mistakes. Trust Me, and watch to see what I will do.

ROMANS 8:28; PROVERBS 11:2; MICAH 7:7

But as for me,

I watch in *hope*

for the LORD, I wait for

God my *Savior*;

my God will hear me.

—MICAH 7:7

COME TO ME FOR UNDERSTANDING since I know you far better than you know yourself. I comprehend you in all your complexity; *no detail of your life is hidden from Me.* I view you through eyes of grace, so don't be afraid of My intimate awareness. Allow the Light of My healing Presence to shine into the deepest recesses of your being—cleansing, healing, refreshing, and renewing you. Trust Me enough to accept the full forgiveness that I offer you continually. This great gift, which cost Me My Life, is yours for all eternity. Forgiveness is at the very core of My abiding Presence. *I will never leave you or forsake you.*

When no one else seems to understand you, simply draw closer to Me. Rejoice in the One who understands you completely and loves you perfectly. As I fill you with My Love, you become a reservoir of love, overflowing into the lives of other people.

PSALM 139:1–4; 2 CORINTHIANS 1:21–22; JOSHUA 1:5

"No one will be able to *stand* up against you all the days of your life. As I was with Moses, so I will be with you; I will *never* leave you nor forsake you."

—Joshua 1:5

COME TO ME when you are weak and weary. Rest snugly in My everlasting arms. I do not despise your weakness, My child. Actually, it draws Me closer to you because weakness stirs up My compassion—My yearning to help. Accept yourself in your weariness, knowing that I understand how difficult your journey has been.

Do not compare yourself with others who seem to skip along their life-paths with ease. Their journeys have been different from yours, and I have gifted them with abundant energy. I have gifted you with fragility, providing opportunities for your spirit to blossom in My Presence. Accept this gift as a sacred treasure: delicate, yet glowing with brilliant Light. Rather than struggling to disguise or deny your weakness, allow Me to bless you richly through it.

ISAIAH 42:3; ISAIAH 54:10; ROMANS 8:26

"Though the mountains be shaken and the hills be removed, yet my *unfailing* love for you will not be shaken nor my covenant of peace be removed," says the LORD, who has *compassion* on you.

—ISAIAH 54:10

LOOK TO ME CONTINUALLY for help, comfort, and companionship. Because I am always by your side, the briefest glance can connect you with Me. When you look to Me for help, it flows freely from My Presence. This recognition of your need for Me, in small matters as well as in large ones, keeps you spiritually alive.

When you need comfort, I love to enfold you in My arms. I enable you not only to feel comforted but also to be a channel through whom I comfort others. Thus you are doubly blessed, because a living channel absorbs some of whatever flows through it.

My constant Companionship is the *pièce de résistance*: the summit of salvation blessings. No matter what losses you experience in your life, no one can take away this glorious gift.

PSALM 34:4–6; PSALM 105:4; 2 CORINTHIANS 1:3–4

Praise be to the God

and Father of our Lord

Jesus Christ, the Father of

compassion and

the God of all comfort, who

comforts us in all our troubles,

so that we can comfort

those in any trouble with the

comfort we ourselves

have received from God.

—2 Corinthians 1:3-4

And we know that in all things God works for the good of those who love him, who have been called according to his purpose.

—Romans 8:28

YOU ARE MINE FOR ALL TIME—and beyond time, into eternity. No power can deny you your inheritance in heaven. I want you to realize how utterly secure you are! Even if you falter as you journey through life, I will never let go of your hand.

Knowing that your future is absolutely assured can free you to live abundantly today. I have prepared this day for you with the most tender concern and attention to detail. Instead of approaching the day as a blank page that you need to fill up, try living it in a responsive mode, being on the lookout for all that I am doing. This sounds easy, but it requires a deep level of trust, based on the knowledge that *My way is perfect*.

1 PETER 1:3–4; PSALM 37:23–24; PSALM 18:30

If the L<small>ORD</small>

delights in a man's

way, he makes his steps

firm; though he stumble,

he will not fall, for the

L<small>ORD</small> *upholds*

him with his hand.

—P<small>SALM</small> 37:23-24

I AM A GOD WHO HEALS. I heal broken bodies, broken minds, broken hearts, broken lives, and broken relationships. My very Presence has immense healing powers. You cannot live close to Me without experiencing some degree of healing. However, it is also true that *you have not because you ask not.* You receive the healing that flows naturally from My Presence, whether you seek it or not. But there is more—much more—available to those who ask.

The first step in receiving healing is to live ever so close to Me. The benefits of this practice are too numerous to list. As you grow more and more intimate with Me, I reveal My will to you more directly. When the time is right, I prompt you to ask for healing of some brokenness in you or in another person. The healing may be instantaneous, or it may be a process. That is up to Me. Your part is to trust Me fully and to thank Me for the restoration that has begun.

I rarely heal all the brokenness in a person's life. Even My servant Paul was told, *"My grace is sufficient for you,"* when he sought healing for the *thorn in his flesh.* Nonetheless, much healing is available to those whose lives are intimately interwoven with Mine. *Ask, and you will receive.*

JAMES 4:2 KJV; 2 CORINTHIANS 12:7–9; MATTHEW 7:7

"Ask and it

will be

given

to you;

seek and

you will

find."

—Matthew 7:7

LET ME SHOW YOU My way for you this day. I guide you continually so you can relax and enjoy My Presence in the present. Living well is both a discipline and an art. Concentrate on staying close to Me, the divine Artist. Discipline your thoughts to trust Me as I work My ways in your life. Pray about everything; then leave outcomes up to Me. Do not fear My will, for through it I accomplish what is best for you. Take a deep breath and dive into the depths of absolute trust in Me. *Underneath are the everlasting arms!*

PSALM 5:2–3; ISAIAH 26:4 AMP; DEUTERONOMY 33:27

Listen to my cry for help,

my King and my God, for

to you I *pray*. In the

morning, O LORD, you hear

my voice; in the morning I lay

my requests before you and

wait in expectation.

—PSALM 5:2-3

DO NOT EXPECT to be treated fairly in this life. People will say and do hurtful things to you, things that you don't deserve. When someone mistreats you, try to view it as an opportunity to grow in grace. See how quickly you can forgive the one who has wounded you. Don't be concerned about setting the record straight. Instead of obsessing about other people's opinions of you, keep your focus on Me. Ultimately, it is My view of you that counts.

As you concentrate on relating to Me, remember that I have clothed you in My righteousness and holiness. I see you attired in these radiant garments, which I bought for you with My blood. This also is not fair; it is pure gift. When others treat you unfairly, remember that My ways with you are much better than fair. My ways are Peace and *Love, which I have poured out into your heart by My Spirit.*

COLOSSIANS 3:13; ISAIAH 61:10;

EPHESIANS 1:7–8; ROMANS 5:5

And hope does not disappoint

us, because God has poured

out his *love* into our

hearts by the Holy Spirit,

whom he has given us.

—Romans 5:5

REST IN ME, MY CHILD. Give your mind a break from planning and trying to anticipate what will happen. *Pray continually*, asking My Spirit to take charge of the details of this day. Remember that you are on a journey with Me. When you try to peer into the future and plan for every possibility, you ignore your constant Companion, who sustains you moment by moment. As you gaze anxiously into the distance, you don't even feel the strong grip of My hand holding yours. How foolish you are, My child!

Remembrance of Me is a daily discipline. Never lose sight of My Presence with you. This will keep you resting in Me all day, every day.

1 THESSALONIANS 5:17;

PSALM 139:9–10 NKJV; PSALM 62:5

If I take the *wings* of
the morning, and dwell in
the uttermost parts of the
sea, even there Your hand
shall *lead* me, and Your
right hand shall hold me.

—Psalm 139:9–10 NKJV

Look to the LORD *and his strength; seek his face always.*

—Psalm 105:4

EVERY TIME YOU AFFIRM YOUR TRUST IN ME, you put a coin into My treasury. Thus you build up equity in preparation for days of trouble. I keep safely in My Heart all trust invested in Me, with interest compounded continuously. The more you trust Me, the more I empower you to do so.

Practice trusting Me during quiet days, when nothing much seems to be happening. Then when storms come, your trust balance will be sufficient to see you through. *Store up for yourself treasure in heaven*, through placing your trust in Me. This practice will keep you in My Peace.

PSALM 33:20–21; PSALM 56:3–4; MATTHEW 6:20–21

When I am afraid,

I will *trust* in you.

In God, whose word I

praise, in God I trust; I will

not be afraid. What can

mortal man do to me?

—Psalm 56:3–4

COME TO ME when you are hurting, and I will soothe your pain. Come to Me when you are joyful, and I will share your Joy, multiplying it many times over. I am All you need, just when you need it. Your deepest desires find fulfillment in Me alone.

This is the age of self-help. Bookstores abound with books about "taking care of number one," making oneself the center of all things. The main goal of these methodologies is to become self-sufficient and confident. You, however, have been called to take a "road less traveled": continual dependence on Me. True confidence comes from knowing you are complete in My Presence. Everything you need has its counterpart in Me.

ISAIAH 49:13; JOHN 15:5; JAMES 1:4

Shout for joy, O heavens;

rejoice, O earth; burst

into song, O mountains!

For the LORD comforts

his people and will have

compassion

on his afflicted ones.

—ISAIAH 49:13

Softly I announce My Presence. Shimmering hues of radiance tap gently at your consciousness, seeking entrance. Though I have all Power in heaven and on earth, I am infinitely tender with you. The weaker you are, the more gently I approach you. Let your weakness be a door to My Presence. Whenever you feel inadequate, remember that I am your *ever-present Help*.

Hope in Me, and you will be protected from depression and self-pity. Hope is like a golden cord connecting you to heaven. The more you cling to this cord, the more I bear the weight of your burdens; thus, you are lightened. Heaviness is not of My kingdom. Cling to hope, and My rays of Light will reach you through the darkness.

PSALM 46:1; ROMANS 12:12; ROMANS 15:13

Be
joyful
in hope,
patient
in affliction,
faithful
in prayer.

—Romans 12:12

COME TO ME AND REST. I am all around you, to bless and restore. Breathe Me in with each breath. The way just ahead of you is very steep. Slow down and cling tightly to My hand. I am teaching you a difficult lesson, learned only by hardship.

Lift up empty hands of faith to receive My precious Presence. Light, Life, Joy, and Peace flow freely through this gift. When your focus turns away from Me, you grasp for other things. You drop the glowing gift of My Presence as you reach for lifeless ashes. Return to Me; regain My Presence.

MATTHEW 11:28–29; 1 TIMOTHY 2:8; ZECHARIAH 1:3

Therefore tell the people: This is what the LORD Almighty says: "*Return* to me," declares the LORD Almighty, "and I will return to you," says the LORD Almighty.

—ZECHARIAH 1:3

REST IN MY RADIANT PRESENCE. The world around you seems to spin faster and faster, till everything is a blur. Yet there is a cushion of calm at the center of your life, where you live in union with Me. Return to this soothing Center as often as you can, for this is where you are energized: filled with My Love, Joy, and Peace.

The world is a needy place; do not go there for sustenance. Instead, come to Me. Learn to depend on Me alone, and your weakness will become saturated with My Power. When you find your completeness in Me, you can help other people without using them to meet your own needs. Live in the Light of My Presence, and your light will shine brightly into the lives of others.

GALATIANS 5:22; 2 CORINTHIANS 12:9; 1 JOHN 4:12

But the fruit of the

Spirit is love, joy,

peace, patience, kindness,

goodness, faithfulness.

—GALATIANS 5:22

*But if from there you seek the
LORD your God, you will find him
if you look for him with all your
heart and with all your soul.*

—Deuteronomy 4:29

COME TO ME with a teachable spirit, eager to be changed. A close walk with Me is a life of continual newness. Do not cling to old ways as you step into a new year. Instead, seek My Face with an open mind, knowing that your journey with Me involves being *transformed by the renewing of your mind*. As you focus your thoughts on Me, be aware that I am fully attentive to you. I see you with a steady eye because My attention span is infinite. I know and understand you completely; My thoughts embrace you in everlasting Love. *I also know the plans I have for you: plans to prosper you and not to harm you, plans to give you hope and a future.* Give yourself fully to this adventure of increasing attentiveness to My Presence.

PSALM 27:8 ESV; ROMANS 12:2; JEREMIAH 29:11

You have said,

"Seek my face." My

heart says to you,

"Your face, LORD, do I seek."

—PSALM 27:8 ESV

TRY TO SEE THINGS more and more from My perspective. Let the Light of My Presence so fully fill your mind that you view the world through Me. When little things don't go as you had hoped, look to Me lightheartedly and say, "Oh, well." This simple discipline can protect you from being burdened with an accumulation of petty cares and frustrations. If you practice this diligently, you will make a life-changing discovery: You realize that most of the things that worry you are not important. If you shrug them off immediately and return your focus to Me, you will walk through your days with lighter steps and a joyful heart.

When serious problems come your way, you will have more reserves for dealing with them. You will not have squandered your energy on petty problems. You may even reach the point where you can agree with the apostle Paul that all your troubles are *light and momentary* compared with *the eternal glory* being achieved by them.

PSALM 36:9 NKJV; PROVERBS 20:24;
2 CORINTHIANS 4:17–18

A man's steps are

directed

by the LORD. How

then can anyone

understand

his own way?

—PROVERBS 20:24

Trust Me, and don't be afraid. Many things feel out of control. Your routines are not running smoothly. You tend to feel more secure when your life is predictable. Let Me lead you to *the rock that is higher than you* and your circumstances. *Take refuge in the shelter of My wings*, where you are absolutely secure.

When you are shaken out of your comfortable routines, grip My hand tightly and look for growth opportunities. Instead of bemoaning the loss of your comfort, accept the challenge of something new. *I lead you on from glory to glory*, making you fit for My kingdom. Say *yes* to the ways I work in your life. Trust Me, and don't be afraid.

Isaiah 12:2; Psalm 61:2–4; 2 Corinthians 3:18 nkjv

From the ends of the earth I

call to you, I call as my heart

grows faint; lead me to

the rock that is higher than I.

For you have been my refuge,

a *strong* tower against

the foe. I long to dwell in your

tent forever and take refuge

in the shelter of your wings.

—Psalm 61:2-4

WORSHIP ME ONLY. I am *King of kings and Lord of lords, dwelling in unapproachable Light.* I am taking care of you! I am not only committed to caring for you, but I am also absolutely capable of doing so. Rest in Me, My weary one, for this is a form of worship.

Though self-flagellation has gone out of style, many of My children drive themselves like racehorses. They whip themselves into action, ignoring how exhausted they are. They forget that I am sovereign and that *My ways are higher* than theirs. Underneath their driven service, they may secretly resent Me as a harsh taskmaster. Their worship of Me is lukewarm because I am no longer their *First Love.*

My invitation never changes: *Come to Me, all you who are weary, and I will give you rest.* Worship Me by resting peacefully in My Presence.

1 TIMOTHY 6:15–16; ISAIAH 55:8–9;
REVELATION 2:4; MATTHEW 11:28

"*Come* to me,

all you who are weary

and burdened, and I

will give you *rest*."

—MATTHEW 11:28

BRING ME YOUR MIND for rest and renewal. Let Me infuse My Presence into your thoughts. As your mind stops racing, your body relaxes and you regain awareness of Me. This awareness is vital to your spiritual well-being; it is your lifeline, spiritually speaking.

There are actually more than four dimensions in this world where you live. In addition to the three dimensions of space and the one of time, there is the dimension of openness to My Presence. This dimension transcends the others, giving you glimpses of heaven while you still reside on earth. This was part of My original design for mankind. Adam and Eve used to walk with Me in the garden, before their expulsion from Eden. I want you to walk with Me in the garden of your heart, where I have taken up permanent residence.

GENESIS 3:8; PSALM 89:15; PROVERBS 4:23

Blessed are those who have learned to *acclaim* you, who walk in the light of your presence, O Lord.

—Psalm 89:15

For nothing is impossible with God.

—Luke 1:37

HOLD MY HAND, and walk joyously with Me through this day. Together we will savor the pleasures and endure the difficulties it brings. Be on the lookout for everything I have prepared for you: stunning scenery, bracing winds of adventure, cozy nooks for resting when you are weary, and much more. I am your Guide, as well as your constant Companion. I know every step of the journey ahead of you, all the way to heaven.

You don't have to choose between staying close to Me and staying on course. Since *I am the Way*, staying close to Me *is* staying on course. As you focus your thoughts on Me, I will guide you carefully along today's journey. Don't worry about what is around the next bend. Just concentrate on enjoying My Presence and staying in step with Me.

PHILIPPIANS 4:13 NKJV; ISAIAH 58:11;
JOHN 14:6; COLOSSIANS 4:2

The Lord will *guide* you always; he will satisfy your needs in a sun-scorched land and will *strengthen* your frame. You will be like a well-watered garden, like a spring whose waters never fail.

—Isaiah 58:11

LEARN TO LIVE above your circumstances. This requires focused time with Me, the *One who overcame the world*. Trouble and distress are woven into the very fabric of this perishing world. Only My Life in you can empower you to face this endless flow of problems with *good cheer*.

As you sit quietly in My Presence, I shine Peace into your troubled mind and heart. Little by little, you are freed from earthly shackles and lifted up above your circumstances. You gain My perspective on your life, enabling you to distinguish between what is important and what is not. Rest in My Presence, *receiving Joy that no one can take away from you*.

JOHN 16:33 NKJV; PSALM 42:5 NASB; JOHN 16:22

"These things I have *spoken* to you, that in Me you may have peace. In the world you will have tribulation; but be of good *cheer*, I have overcome the world."

—John 16:33 NKJV

BRING ME ALL YOUR FEELINGS, even the ones you wish you didn't have. Fear and anxiety still plague you. Feelings per se are not sinful, but they can be temptations to sin. Blazing missiles of fear fly at you day and night; these attacks from the evil one come at you relentlessly. Use your *shield of faith to extinguish those flaming arrows.* Affirm your trust in Me, regardless of how you feel. If you persist, your feelings will eventually fall in line with your faith.

Do not hide from your fear or pretend it isn't there. Anxiety that you hide in the recesses of your heart will give birth to fear of fear: a monstrous mutation. Bring your anxieties out into the Light of My Presence, where we can deal with them together. Concentrate on trusting Me, and fearfulness will gradually lose its foothold within you.

EPHESIANS 6:16; 1 JOHN 1:5–7; ISAIAH 12:2

Surely God is my salvation; I will *trust* and not be afraid. The LORD, the LORD, is my *strength* and my song; he has become my salvation.

—Isaiah 12:2

SIT QUIETLY WITH ME, letting all your fears and worries bubble up to the surface of your consciousness. There, in the Light of My Presence, the bubbles pop and disappear. However, some fears surface over and over again, especially fear of the future. You tend to project yourself mentally into the next day, week, month, year, decade; and you visualize yourself coping badly in those times. What you are seeing is a false image because it doesn't include Me. Those gloomy times that you imagine will not come to pass since My Presence will be with you at *all* times.

When a future-oriented worry assails you, capture it and disarm it by suffusing the Light of My Presence into that mental image. Say to yourself, "Jesus will be with me then and there. With His help, I can cope!" Then, come home to the present moment, where you can enjoy Peace in My Presence.

LUKE 12:22–25; DEUTERONOMY 31:6;
2 CORINTHIANS 10:5

Be *strong* and
courageous. Do not be afraid
or terrified because of them,
for the Lᴏʀᴅ your God goes
with you; he will *never*
leave you nor forsake you.

—Dᴇᴜᴛᴇʀᴏɴᴏᴍʏ 31:6

SEEK ME with your whole being. I desire to be found by you, and I orchestrate the events of your life with that purpose in mind. When things go well and you are blessed, you can feel Me smiling on you. When you encounter rough patches along your life-journey, trust that My Light is still shining upon you. My reasons for allowing these adversities may be shrouded in mystery, but My continual Presence with you is an absolute promise. Seek Me in good times; seek Me in hard times. You will find Me watching over you all the time.

DEUTERONOMY 4:29; HEBREWS 10:23;
PSALM 145:20; PSALM 121:7–8

Let us hold

unswervingly to the

hope we profess,

for he who

promised

is faithful.

—HEBREWS 10:23

"So do not fear, for I am with you; do not be dismayed, for I am your God. I will strengthen you and help you; I will uphold you with my righteous right hand."

—Isaiah 41:10

I AM YOUR REFUGE AND STRENGTH, an ever-present Help in trouble. Therefore, you don't need to be afraid of anything—not even cataclysmic circumstances. The media are increasingly devoted to fear-inducing subject matter: terrorism, serial killers, environmental catastrophes. If you focus on such dangers and forget that I am your Refuge in all circumstances, you will become increasingly fearful. Every day I manifest My grace in countless places and situations, but the media take no notice. I shower not only blessings but also out-right miracles on your planet.

As you grow closer to Me, I open your eyes to see more and more of My Presence all around you. Things that most people hardly notice, like shifting shades of sunlight, fill you with heart-bursting Joy. You have eyes that see and ears that hear, so proclaim My abiding Presence in the world.

PSALM 46:1–3; PSALM 89:15–16

God is our refuge and strength, an ever-present *help* in trouble. Therefore we will not fear, though the earth give way and the mountains fall into the heart of the sea, though its waters roar and foam and the mountains quake with their surging.

—Psalm 46:1–3

LEARN TO LAUGH at yourself more freely. Don't take yourself or your circumstances so seriously. Relax and know that I am *God with you*. When you desire My will above all else, life becomes much less threatening. Stop trying to monitor My responsibilities—things that are beyond your control. Find freedom by accepting the boundaries of your domain.

Laughter lightens your load and lifts your heart into heavenly places. Your laughter rises to heaven and blends with angelic melodies of praise. Just as parents delight in the laughter of their children, so I delight in hearing My children laugh. I rejoice when you trust Me enough to enjoy your life lightheartedly.

Do not miss the Joy of My Presence by carrying the weight of the world on your shoulders. Rather, *take My yoke upon you and learn from Me. My yoke is comfortable and pleasant; My burden is light and easily borne.*

PROVERBS 17:22; PROVERBS 31:25;
MATTHEW 1:23; MATTHEW 11:29–30 AMP

A *cheerful* heart

is good medicine,

but a crushed spirit

dries up the bones.

—PROVERBS 17:22

DO NOT HESITATE TO RECEIVE JOY FROM ME, for I bestow it on you abundantly. The more you rest in My Presence, the more freely My blessings flow into you. In the Light of My Love, you are gradually *transformed from glory to glory*. It is through spending time with Me that you realize *how wide and long and high and deep is My Love for you.*

Sometimes the relationship I offer you seems too good to be true. I pour My very Life into you, and all you have to do is receive Me. In a world characterized by working and taking, the admonition to rest and receive seems too easy. There is a close connection between receiving and believing: As you trust Me more and more, you are able to receive Me and My blessings abundantly. *Be still, and know that I am God.*

2 CORINTHIANS 3:18 NASB;
EPHESIANS 3:17–19; PSALM 46:10

But we all, with unveiled face, beholding as in a mirror the *glory* of the Lord, are being transformed into the same image from glory to glory, just as from the Lord, the Spirit.

—2 CORINTHIANS 3:18 NASB

LET MY LOVE seep into the inner recesses of your being. Do not close off any part of yourself from Me. I know you inside and out, so do not try to present a "cleaned-up" self to Me. Wounds that you shut away from the Light of My Love will fester and become wormy. Secret sins that you "hide" from Me can split off and develop lives of their own, controlling you without your realizing it.

Open yourself fully to My transforming Presence. Let My brilliant Love-Light search out and destroy hidden fears. This process requires time alone with Me, as My Love soaks into your innermost being. Enjoy *My perfect Love, which expels every trace of fear.*

PSALM 139:1–4, 23–24; 1 JOHN 4:18 AMP

O LORD, you have searched me and you know me. You know when I sit and when I rise; you perceive my thoughts from afar. You discern my going out and my lying down; you are familiar with all my ways. Before a word is on my tongue you know it completely, O LORD. . . . *Search* me, O God, and know my heart; test me and know my anxious thoughts. See if there is any offensive way in me, and lead me in the way everlasting.

—PSALM 139:1-4, 23-24

I, THE CREATOR OF THE UNIVERSE, am with you and for you. What more could you need? When you feel some lack, it is because you are not connecting with Me at a deep level. I offer abundant Life; your part is to trust Me, refusing to worry about anything.

It is not so much adverse events that make you anxious as it is your thoughts about those events. Your mind engages in efforts to take control of a situation, to bring about the result you desire. Your thoughts close in on the problem like ravenous wolves. Determined to make things go your way, you forget that I am in charge of your life. The only remedy is to switch your focus from the problem to My Presence. Stop all your striving, and watch to see what I will do. *I am the Lord!*

ROMANS 8:31–32; MICAH 7:7; 1 CORINTHIANS 12:3

What, then, shall we say in response to this? If God is for us, *who* can be against us? He who did not spare his own Son, but *gave* him up for us all—how will he not also, along with him, graciously give us all things?

—ROMANS 8:31-32

Because you are my help, I sing in the shadow of your wings. My soul clings to you; your right hand upholds me.

—Psalm 63:7–8

I AM LEADING YOU, STEP BY STEP, through your life. Hold My hand in trusting dependence, letting Me guide you through this day. Your future looks uncertain and feels flimsy—even precarious. That is how it should be. *Secret things belong to the Lord*, and future things are secret things. When you try to figure out the future, you are grasping at things that are Mine. This, like all forms of worry, is an act of rebellion: doubting My promises to care for you.

Whenever you find yourself worrying about the future, repent and return to Me. I will show you the next step forward, and the one after that, and the one after that. Relax and enjoy the journey in My Presence, trusting Me to open up the way before you as you go.

DEUTERONOMY 29:29; LUKE 12:25–26; PSALM 32:8

I will instruct you and *teach* you in the

way you should go; I

will *counsel* you

and watch over you.

—Psalm 32:8

REST IN THE STILLNESS of My Presence while I prepare you for this day. Let the radiance of My Glory shine upon you as you wait on Me in confident trust. *Be still, and know that I am God.* There is both a passive and an active side to trusting Me. As you rest in My Presence, focusing on Me, I quietly build bonds of trust between us. When you respond to the circumstances of your life with affirmations of trust, you actively participate in this process.

I am always with you, so you have no reason to be afraid. Your fear often manifests itself in excessive planning. Your mind is so accustomed to this pattern of thinking that you are only now becoming aware of how pervasive it is and how much it hinders your intimacy with Me. Repent of this tendency and resist it whenever you realize you are wandering down this well-worn path. Return to My Presence, which always awaits you in the present moment. I accept you back with *no condemnation.*

PSALM 46:10; ROMANS 8:1–2

"Be still, and know

that I am God;

I will be

exalted

among the nations,

I will be exalted

in the earth."

—PSALM 46:10

SEEK MY FACE more and more. You are really just beginning your journey of intimacy with Me. It is not an easy road, but it is a delightful and privileged way: a treasure hunt. I am the Treasure, and the Glory of My Presence glistens and shimmers along the way. Hardships are part of the journey too. I mete them out ever so carefully, in just the right dosage, with a tenderness you can hardly imagine. Do not recoil from afflictions since they are among My most favored gifts. *Trust Me and don't be afraid, for I am your Strength and Song.*

PSALM 27:8 NKJV; 2 CORINTHIANS 4:7–8; ISAIAH 12:2

But we have this

treasure in jars of

clay to show that this

all-surpassing power is

from God and not from us.

We are hard pressed on

every side, but not crushed;

perplexed, but not in despair.

—2 CORINTHIANS 4:7–8

MAKE ME YOUR FOCAL POINT as you move through this day. Just as a spinning ballerina must keep returning her eyes to a given point to maintain her balance, so you must keep returning your focus to Me. Circumstances are in flux, and the world seems to be whirling around you. The only way to keep your balance is to *fix your eyes on Me*, the One who never changes. If you gaze too long at your circumstances, you will become dizzy and confused. Look to Me, refreshing yourself in My Presence, and your steps will be steady and sure.

HEBREWS 12:2; PSALM 102:27; 1 JOHN 3:19–20

This then is how we know

that we *belong* to

the truth, and how we set

our hearts at rest in his

presence whenever our hearts

condemn us. For God is

greater than our hearts,

and he knows everything.

—1 JOHN 3:19–20

TRUST ME ONE DAY AT A TIME. This keeps you close to Me, responsive to My will. Trust is not a natural response, especially for those who have been deeply wounded. My Spirit within you is your resident Tutor, helping you in this supernatural endeavor. Yield to His gentle touch; be sensitive to His prompting.

Exert your will to trust Me in all circumstances. Don't let your need to understand distract you from My Presence. I will equip you to get through this day victoriously as you live in deep dependence on Me. *Tomorrow is busy worrying about itself; don't get tangled up in its worry-webs.* Trust Me one day at a time.

PSALM 84:12; 1 CORINTHIANS 6:19;
JEREMIAH 17:7 NKJV; MATTHEW 6:34

"Blessed is

the man who

trusts

in the LORD,

and whose hope

is the LORD."

—JEREMIAH 17:7 NKJV

The LORD is near to all who call upon Him, to all who call upon Him in truth.

—Psalm 145:18 NKJV

SELF-PITY IS A SLIMY, BOTTOMLESS PIT. Once you fall in, you tend to go deeper and deeper into the mire. As you slide down those slippery walls, you are well on your way to depression, and the darkness is profound.

Your only hope is to look up and see the Light of My Presence shining down on you. Though the Light looks dim from your perspective, deep in the pit, those rays of hope can reach you at any depth. While you focus on Me in trust, you rise ever so slowly out of the abyss of despair. Finally, you can reach up and grasp My hand. I will pull you out into the Light again. I will gently cleanse you, washing off the clinging mire. I will cover you with My righteousness and walk with you down the path of Life.

PSALM 40:2–3; PSALM 42:5 NASB; PSALM 147:11

He lifted me out of the slimy

pit, out of the mud and mire;

he set my feet on a rock

and gave me a *firm*

place to stand. He put a

new song in my mouth, a

hymn of praise to our God.

Many will see and fear and

put their trust in the LORD.

—PSALM 40:2-3

DRAW NEAR TO ME with a thankful heart, aware that your cup is overflowing with blessings. Gratitude enables you to perceive Me more clearly and to rejoice in our Love-relationship. *Nothing can separate you from My loving Presence*! That is the basis of your security. Whenever you start to feel anxious, remind yourself that your security rests in Me alone, and I am totally trustworthy.

You will never be in control of your life circumstances, but you can relax and trust in My control. Instead of striving for a predictable, safe lifestyle, seek to know Me in greater depth and breadth. I long to make your life a glorious adventure, but you must stop clinging to old ways. I am always doing something new within My beloved ones. Be on the lookout for all that I have prepared for you.

ROMANS 8:38–39; PSALM 56:3–4; ISAIAH 43:19

"See, I am doing a new thing!

Now it *springs*

up; do you not perceive it?

I am making a way in the

desert and *streams*

in the wasteland."

—Isaiah 43:19

LEARN TO RELATE to others through My Love rather than yours. Your human love is ever so limited, full of flaws and manipulation. My loving Presence, which always enfolds you, is available to bless others as well as you. Instead of trying harder to help people through your own paltry supplies, become aware of My unlimited supply, which is accessible to you continually. Let My Love envelop your outreach to other people.

Many of My precious children have fallen prey to burnout. A better description of their condition might be "drainout." Countless interactions with needy people have drained them, without their conscious awareness. You are among these weary ones, who are like wounded soldiers needing R & R. Take time to rest in the Love-Light of My Presence. I will gradually restore to you the energy that you have lost over the years. *Come to Me, all you who are weary and burdened, and you will find rest for your souls.*

PSALM 36:5; EXODUS 33:14; MATTHEW 11:28–29

Your love, O LORD,

reaches to the

heavens,

your faithfulness

to the skies.

—PSALM 36:5

YOU CAN LIVE as close to Me as you choose. I set up no barriers between us; neither do I tear down barriers that you erect.

People tend to think their circumstances determine the quality of their lives. So they pour their energy into trying to control those situations. They feel happy when things are going well and sad or frustrated when things don't turn out as they'd hoped. They rarely question this correlation between their circumstances and feelings. Yet it is possible *to be content in any and every situation*.

Put more energy into trusting Me and enjoying My Presence. Don't let your well-being depend on your circumstances. Instead, connect your joy to My precious promises:

I am with you and will watch over you wherever
you go. I will meet all your needs according
to My glorious riches. Nothing in all creation
will be able to separate you from My Love.

PHILIPPIANS 4:12; GENESIS 28:15;
PHILIPPIANS 4:19; ROMANS 8:38–39

I have learned the

secret of being

content in any

and every situation.

—PHILIPPIANS 4:12

STAY CALMLY CONSCIOUS OF ME today, no matter what. Remember that I go before you as well as with you into the day. Nothing takes Me by surprise. I will not allow circumstances to overwhelm you so long as you look to Me. I will help you cope with whatever the moment presents. Collaborating with Me brings *blessings that far outweigh all your troubles.* Awareness of My Presence contains Joy that can endure all eventualities.

PSALM 23:1–4 NKJV;

2 CORINTHIANS 4:16–17; PSALM 28:7

Therefore we do not lose heart.

Though outwardly we are wasting

away, yet inwardly we are being

renewed day by day. For

our light and momentary troubles

are achieving for us an eternal

glory that far outweighs them all.

—2 Corinthians 4:16–17

As for God, his way is perfect;
the word of the LORD is
flawless. He is a shield for
all who take refuge in him.

—*Psalm 18:30*

I AM WORKING ON YOUR BEHALF. Bring Me all your concerns, including your dreams. Talk with Me about everything, letting the Light of My Presence shine on your hopes and plans. Spend time allowing My Light to infuse your dreams with life, gradually transforming them into reality. This is a very practical way of collaborating with Me. I, the Creator of the universe, have deigned to cocreate with you. Do not try to hurry this process. If you want to work with Me, you have to accept My time frame. Hurry is not in My nature. Abraham and Sarah had to wait many years for the fulfillment of My promise, a son. How their long wait intensified their enjoyment of this child! *Faith is the assurance of things hoped for, perceiving as real fact what is not revealed to the senses.*

PSALM 36:9; GENESIS 21:1–7; HEBREWS 11:1 AMP

For with you is the

fountain of life; in your

light we see light.

—Psalm 36:9

COME TO ME FOR REST and refreshment. The journey has been too much for you, and you are bone-weary. Do not be ashamed of your exhaustion. Instead, see it as an opportunity for Me to take charge of your life.

Remember that *I can fit everything into a pattern for good*, including the things you wish were different. Start with where you are at this point in time and space, accepting that this is where I intend you to be. You will get through today one step, one moment at a time. Your main responsibility is to remain attentive to Me, letting Me guide you through the many choices along your pathway.

This sounds like an easy assignment, but it is not. Your desire to live in My Presence goes against the grain of the world, the flesh, and the devil. Much of your weariness results from your constant battle against these opponents. However, you are on the path of My choosing, so do not give up! *Hope in Me, for you will again praise Me for the help of My Presence.*

ROMANS 8:28 AMP; PSALM 42:5 NASB

Why are you in despair, O

my soul? And why have you

become disturbed within

me? Hope in God, for I shall

again *praise* Him for

the help of His presence.

—Psalm 42:5 NASB

YOU CAN ACHIEVE THE VICTORIOUS LIFE through living in deep dependence on Me. People usually associate victory with success: not falling or stumbling, not making mistakes. But those who are successful in their own strength tend to go their own way, forgetting about Me. It is through problems and failure, weakness and neediness, that you learn to rely on Me.

True dependence is not simply asking Me to bless what you have decided to do. It is coming to Me with an open mind and heart, inviting Me to plant My desires within you. I may infuse within you a dream that seems far beyond your reach. You know that in yourself you cannot achieve such a goal. Thus begins your journey of profound reliance on Me. It is a faith-walk, taken one step at a time, leaning on Me as much as you need. This is not a path of continual success but of multiple failures. However, each failure is followed by a growth spurt, nourished by increased reliance on Me. Enjoy the blessedness of a victorious life through deepening your dependence on Me.

PSALM 34:17–18; 2 CORINTHIANS 5:7 NKJV

The righteous cry out, and the Lord hears them; he *delivers* them from all their troubles. The Lord is close to the brokenhearted and *saves* those who are crushed in spirit.

—Psalm 34:17–18

LINGER IN MY PRESENCE A WHILE. Rein in your impulses to plunge into the day's activities. Beginning your day alone with Me is essential preparation for success. A great athlete takes time to prepare himself mentally for the feat ahead of him before he moves a muscle. Similarly, your time of being still in My Presence equips you for the day ahead of you. Only I know what will happen to you this day. I have arranged the events you will encounter as you go along your way. If you are not adequately equipped for the journey, you will *grow weary and lose heart*. Relax with Me while I ready you for action.

ZECHARIAH 2:13; EPHESIANS 2:10; HEBREWS 12:3

For we are God's workmanship, *created* in Christ Jesus to do good works, which God prepared in advance for us to do.

—Ephesians 2:10

REST IN MY PRESENCE, allowing Me to take charge of this day. Do not bolt into the day like a racehorse suddenly released. Instead, walk purposefully with Me, letting Me direct your course one step at a time. Thank Me for each blessing along the way; this brings Joy to both you and Me. A grateful heart protects you from negative thinking. Thankfulness enables you to see the abundance I shower upon you daily. Your prayers and petitions are winged into heaven's throne room when they are permeated with thanksgiving. *In everything give thanks, for this is My will for you.*

MATTHEW 11:28 NKJV; COLOSSIANS 4:2;
1 THESSALONIANS 5:18 NASB

Devote yourselves to

prayer,

being watchful and

thankful.

—Colossians 4:2

The LORD replied, "My Presence will go with you, and I will give you rest."

—*Exodus 33:14*

Never take for granted My intimate nearness. Marvel at the wonder of My continual Presence with you. Even the most ardent human lover cannot be with you always. Nor can another person know the intimacies of your heart, mind, and spirit. *I know everything about you—even the number of hairs on your head.* You don't need to work at revealing yourself to Me.

Many people spend a lifetime or a small fortune searching for someone who understands them. Yet I am freely available to all who call upon My Name, who open their hearts to receive Me as Savior. This simple act of faith is the beginning of a lifelong love story. I, the Lover of your soul, understand you perfectly and love you eternally.

PSALM 145:18 NKJV; LUKE 12:7;
JOHN 1:12; ROMANS 10:13

"Indeed, the very hairs of your head are all numbered. Don't be afraid; you are *worth* more than many sparrows."

—Luke 12:7

BE WILLING TO GO OUT on a limb with Me. If that is where I am leading you, it is the safest place to be. Your desire to live a risk-free life is a form of unbelief. Your longing to live close to Me is at odds with your attempts to minimize risk. You are approaching a crossroads in your journey. In order to follow Me wholeheartedly, you must relinquish your tendency to play it safe.

Let Me lead you step by step through this day. If your primary focus is on Me, you can walk along perilous paths without being afraid. Eventually, you will learn to relax and enjoy the adventure of our journey together. As long as you stay close to Me, My sovereign Presence protects you wherever you go.

PSALM 23:4; PSALM 9:10; JOHN 12:26

Those who know your name

will *trust* in you,

for you, Lord, have never

forsaken those who seek you.

—Psalm 9:10

HOLD MY HAND—AND TRUST. So long as you are conscious of My Presence with you, all is well. It is virtually impossible to stumble while walking in the Light with Me. I designed you to enjoy Me above all else. You find the deepest fulfillment of your heart in Me alone.

Fearful, anxious thoughts melt away in the Light of My Presence. When you turn away from Me, you are vulnerable to the darkness that is always at work in the world. Don't be surprised by how easily you sin when you forget to cling to My hand. In the world, dependency is seen as immaturity. But in My kingdom, dependence on Me is a prime measure of maturity.

ISAIAH 41:10; EPHESIANS 5:8 NKJV; PSALM 62:5–6

Find rest, O my soul, in God

alone; my hope comes from

him. He *alone* is my rock

and my salvation; he is my

fortress, I will not be shaken.

—Psalm 62:5-6

REFUSE TO WORRY! In this world there will always be something enticing you to worry. That is the nature of a fallen, fractured planet: Things are not as they should be. So the temptation to be anxious is constantly with you, trying to worm its way into your mind. The best defense is *continual communication with Me, richly seasoned with thanksgiving.* Awareness of My Presence fills your mind with Light and Peace, leaving no room for fear. This awareness lifts you up above your circumstances, enabling you to see problems from My perspective. Live close to Me! Together we can keep the wolves of worry at bay.

LUKE 12:25–26; 1 THESSALONIANS 5:16–18; PSALM 36:9

"Who of you by worrying

can *add* a single hour to

his life? Since you cannot do

this very little thing, why do

you worry about the rest?"

—Luke 12:25-26

Pour all of your energy into trusting Me. It is through trust that you stay connected to Me, aware of My Presence. Every step on your life-journey can be a step of faith. Baby steps of trust are simple for you; you can take them with almost unconscious ease. Giant steps are another matter altogether: leaping across chasms in semi-darkness, scaling cliffs of uncertainty, trudging *through the valley of the shadow of death*. These feats require sheer concentration, as well as utter commitment to Me.

Each of My children is a unique blend of temperament, giftedness, and life experiences. Something that is a baby step for you may be a giant step for another person and vice versa. Only I know the difficulty or ease of each segment of your journey. Beware of trying to impress others by acting as if your giant steps are only baby ones. Do not judge others who hesitate in trembling fear before an act that would be easy for you. If each of My children would seek to please Me above all else, fear of others' judgments would vanish, as would attempts to impress others. Focus your attention on the path just ahead of you and on the One who never leaves your side.

Psalm 23:4; Matthew 7:1–2; Proverbs 29:25

Fear of man will

prove to be a snare,

but whoever *trusts*

in the LORD is kept safe.

—PROVERBS 29:25

"For I know the plans I have for you," declares the LORD, "plans to prosper you and not to harm you, plans to give you hope and a future."

—Jeremiah 29:11